Also by Evelyn McFarlane & James Saywell

If... (Questions for the Game of Life)

If^2... (500 New Questions for the Game of Life)

If^3... (Questions for the Game of Love)

If... Questions for the Soul

How Far Will You Go?

If... Questions for Parents

Would You?

If... Questions for Teens

I Do... Questions for the Biggest Day of Your Life

IF YOU HAD
A MILLION
DOLLARS...

IF YOU HAD A MILLION DOLLARS...

Questions About Your Money and Your Life

Evelyn McFarlane & James Saywell

Villard / New York

Published in the United States by Villard Books, an imprint of The Random House Publishing Group, a division of Random House, Inc., New York.

VILLARD BOOKS and VILLARD & "V" CIRCLED DESIGN are registered trademarks of Random House, Inc.

Library of Congress Cataloging-in-Publication Data
McFarlane, Evelyn.
If you had a million dollars–: questions about your money and your life /
Evelyn McFarlane & James Saywell.
p.   cm.
ISBN 978–0-345–50495–1 (hardcover : alk. paper)
1. Finance, Personal.   2. Money.   I. Saywell, James.   II. Title.
HG179.M246   2008
332.024–dc22   2008044222

Printed in the United States of America on acid-free paper

www.villard.com

2 4 6 8 9 7 5 3 1

First Edition

Book design by Maria Elias

Dedicated to Sandy, there from the beginning

Introduction

If you had a million dollars...It is the classic question and we never get tired of answering it.

Money...it invades every corner of our lives...or does it?

Should it? Can we escape it? Is it a force for good or for evil? Does it corrupt us or motivate us? Can we resist it, live without it? Do we all want more of it? How much is enough?

Money...no matter how much or how little we have, plays a central role in our lives. We think it can solve our problems, and make our dreams come true. We envy those with lots, pity those with little. We fantasize about having much more, and feel guilty when we do. We love talking about it. We boast about bargains, we relish our frivolous purchases, we make sure people know when we have money, and we pretend to have more of it when we don't. We claim it is not the most important thing in life, but can't get it off our minds.

One way or another, money connects to everything we do and much of what we think. This book explores money, with thought, discussion, and fun and provoking questions that get at what this strange and pervasive stuff (money) really means.

Money . . . POWERFUL, *dirty,* LIBERATING, *sexy,* CORRUPTING, ENABLING, *distracting,* FOCUSING, GIVING, *taking,* MEANINGLESS, INESCAPABLE, TEMPTING, *testing,* GROTESQUE, GREAT, DISGUSTING, *alluring.* Money: just may be the craziest, most powerful thing mankind has ever invented. It's time you learned what you really think about it.

IF YOU HAD A MILLION DOLLARS...

Is money freedom?

If your loved one gave you a very expensive
anniversary gift that you hated, what would you do?

Your parents tell you that they are leaving most
of their estate to your sibling(s) and much less to you.
How do you handle it?

Your parents have just told you they are going to spend
all the money they can before dying, and leave the
remainder to charity. What do you say?

A good friend owes you money and has not paid you back for a while. It is not enough to break the bank, but enough to compromise the friendship.
How do you deal with it?

If your boyfriend never let you treat on a night out, how would you feel about it?

What is your definition of personally being debt free?

What minimum amount of money would make a real
change in your lifestyle?

Do you act differently around rich people?

If a good friend came to you for financial help,
what would you do?

What will be your next purchase to keep up
with the Joneses?

What material object brings you the most pleasure?

What material possession do you show off
the most with?

What defines the biggest bang for the buck for you?

Do you find bargaining demeaning, or fun?

What one thing are you stingy about spending on,
even though you do not need to be?

What is the most you would pay for a great meal
in a restaurant?

What is the most you would spend on a first date with someone you really wanted to impress?

What drives you nuts about your bank?

P

When has having a credit card saved you?

Sh

On your deathbed, what will you say is the most
valuable thing you spent your money on?

What is the ideal amount of money you should save
as a percentage of your salary?

What expense catches you by surprise every year?

What expense would you never charge to your
credit card?

If you only lived on cash, with no access to credit,
how would your life change?

What profession gets paid the least
to do the most?

*

What profession gets paid the most
to do the least?

A colleague of yours often takes home office supplies
for personal use at home. Do you care?

If you were given an amount of money with the chance
to leave the country and never come back, even to visit,
how much money would it take to tempt you?

Do you think there should be a salary cap for CEOs
linked to the percentage of what the workers make?

What would you set as minimum wage if you were
given the power to do so?

How much more would you pay for a product
knowing that it was truly manufactured
in the U.S.A.?

What one thing influences you most when deciding
whether to give someone a handout on the street?

If you made more money than you do right now,
would you give more money to charity?

What percentage of people's salary do you think
should be given to charities?

Do you agree that money makes the world go around?

What percentage of you works to make money,
and what percentage works for enjoyment?

Who defines the term "never satisfied" when it
comes to making money?

Who in your family would you treat differently if you
suddenly became rich? Or bankrupt?

Who in your family would treat *you* differently
if you became a millionaire?

When do you tell people what you earn,
and when do you prefer not to?

P

At what point in a relationship are you ready to tell
someone how much money you are worth?

Sh

Below what salary would you be embarrassed
to tell people you earn?

How many times a day do you think
about money?

ريال

Which do think about more often:
sex or money?

WASHINGTON

If you could change your loved one's attitude
toward money, what would you change?

When has money turned you ugly?

How much faith do you have in the stock market?

When has a so-called safe investment for you
not been safe at all?

True or false: money and your sex life are linked.

What salary would you say defines lower, middle, and upper class, and where do you fit in?

What was the best advice you have ever given someone regarding money or investments?

When has money mattered to you most?

How much would it take to make you feel rich?

f

What amount of money would it take to make
you feel financially secure?

What do you see as the biggest waste
of taxpayers' money? And the best spent?

At work they accidentally pay you two months' salary for
one month, and it goes unnoticed. What do you do?

What was the best investment you ever made?

Who has the golden touch with money?

Who of your friends do you suspect is a
house of cards with regards to their finances?

When in life do you feel richest?
And when poorest?

What is your yearly limit on what you can spend
on clothes?

Finish the phrase: Thanks to money
I am happy when . . .

At what age do you think children should be
put on an allowance?

You get to decide what everyone should earn at work.
What fair salaries do you pay people?

Has a bribe ever eased the way for you?

What would you be willing to take a bribe for?

How much would you be willing to lose
gambling in a single night?

Should parents be obliged to pay for their kids'
college education?

If you could ask Suze Orman advice on one thing,
what would it be?

Your pet is sick and the cost for the cure is one
month's salary. Do you spend it?

You are given the option of a 4 1/2-day workweek for
a 10 percent reduction in salary. Do you take it?

Your in-laws will buy you an apartment in a two-family
home if they can live in the attached apartment.
Do you accept?

What is the worst case of money ruining someone
you know?

When have you seen money make someone's
dreams come true?

Who spends the most on frivolous things,
you or your spouse?

Who between you and your spouse has the best attitude toward money?

Where is the line between taking advantage of things at work and stealing?

What is the biggest thing you ever stole?

You notice a $250 credit into your bank account that is a mistake. The bank does not catch it. Do you say something?

You open the door and find a box with your name on it and $50,000 inside, all in $100 bills. What do you do with it?

Someone twice your age wants to pay you to sleep
with them. What is your price?

P

For you money is no object when it comes to what?

Sh

In what way is money "power" in your life?

ريال

What would you pay to have a private dinner with
the next president?

How does the amount of money you thought you were going to earn when you were younger compare to the amount of money you earn now?

You win the lottery. Your loved one says you must give it all to charity or it will destroy your life. What do you do?

You buy your loved one an expensive gift from Tiffany's. They return it, giving you back the money, saying it was too expensive. What do you say?

What do you and your boyfriend/girlfriend most agree on when it comes to deciding how to spend money?

What one thing are you saving for and planning
to buy as soon as possible?

S

Yes or No. Do you spend your money wisely?

Y

When do you tip big?

B

When is a brand worth the extra price?

Where would you hide cash in the house if you wanted to thwart robbers?

When is time truly money for you?

How would you respond to the statement, "poverty is inevitable in this world"?

When are you most hypocritical when it comes to money and spending?

At work you have the option to be a part owner by taking stock options, profiting in good times, losing in bad. What do you do?

You have been given a year to try to make a
million dollars. Your best chance of succeeding
would be to do what?

What amount of money would convince you
to give up your career?

What amount of money would persuade you to
give up your favorite hobby/sport forever?

What is your best idea yet for making money
on the Web?

What activity that does not require spending money
do you enjoy most? The second most?

If you lost your job today, what would be the first
expense you would cut out of your budget?

How much time would you estimate you spend
shopping for items other than groceries?

Does being rich equal being successful?

Do you think parents should provide unconditional financial support for their children?

بلی

Do you believe children, later in life, should support their parents?

If you suddenly came into BIG money, would you tell everyone? Who first?

E

If you lost everything unexpectedly, how would you set out to rebuild your assets?

Do you believe in graduated taxation or a flat tax?

If a rich person gives nothing to charity at all,
do you think less of them?

You win ten million dollars—what do you do with it?

You win one hundred thousand dollars—what do
you do with it?

Do you believe that anyone can get rich
if they try hard enough?

If you had to smuggle $100,000 cash out of the country, how would you do it?

If you were Bill Gates, what would you do with your money to change the world?

What store (other than the grocery store) do you think you have spent the most money in overall in life?

You overhear a stock tip you were not supposed to be privy to. Do you invest?

What problem in your life could be solved
with $500?

R

How much would you be willing to spend to look
ten years younger?

H

What designer label have you paid more for even
though you know the product is no better than
what you had been using?

When has throwing your money around helped you to
get what you wanted? When has it gotten you nowhere?
And when has it backfired?

F

Who is your business hero?

Whose money are you not envious of?

What is the most money you have lost?
And most found?

If you had enough money to buy land and build
your own house, where would it be and what
would it be like?

What one value regarding money do you want to
pass on to your children?

What is the biggest con someone pulled on you?

If you could have a shopping spree in any store,
which would you choose?

You are shopping in a store and walk out with a bagful
of items. At home you discover you have not been
charged for one of the items. What do you do?

Is displaying wealth tacky?

WASHINGTON

A drunk driver has injured you. You can take an out-of-court settlement for money, or send the driver to jail, but not both. Which do you choose?

Who that you know is frugal to a fault?

What money-type person could you never live with?

Could you be happy being the sole breadwinner if you and your spouse decided not to have children?

If you were to convert all your savings into one
other currency, which would you choose?

Who that you know acts rich even though they are not,
and who acts poor when they truly are not?

If you were to make the laws regarding how much
employers would be required to pay for health care,
what would they be?

Someone offers you a million dollars to marry them solely for a green card. It requires you to live with them and do all things necessary to make sure it comes through. Do you do it?

If you could change one aspect of your spending habits, what would you change?

Ego purchase—what's your latest?

What catalog gets you to spend money every time?

What is the most you have spent on a gift
for a friend?

What is the biggest tip you ever gave someone?

What is the most you would pay to splurge for a quality
bottle of wine?

What are you willing to pay more for because it
helps the environment?

Who is the first person you would ask for money
if you needed a large loan?

P

Your boss asks you to tell him/her what you think you
deserve for your Christmas bonus. What do you say?

Sh

Have you ever been poor, but happy, in life?

If given the power, what luxury item would you heavily
tax to help reduce the national debt?

E

Should the interest rates for credit cards be
capped by law?

Would you live in a third-world country solely
because on your money, you could live much better?

L

If you could earn double pay for overtime, would you
work Saturdays and Sundays?

S

In what ways are you smarter than your partner
when it comes to money?

When it comes to money and your boyfriend/girlfriend, on what have you always had to compromise?

When have you been most grateful that you spent the money to get insurance?

When was the closest you came to becoming truly rich?

When was the closest you came to becoming truly rich?

What is the best rags-to-riches story you know of someone personally?

When you die, how much money do you hope
to have in the bank?

When have you accepted money and then regretted it
because of the strings attached?

How much money would you leave to your pet
when you die?

Who should have all their money taken away?

You discover that your spouse is secretly gambling away your savings. What do you do to protect yourself financially?

You discover that your spouse has been seriously cheating on your taxes that you file jointly. What do you do?

Who is truly penny-wise and pound-foolish?

When have you made "easy money"?

Would you like to have a sugar daddy or sugar momma?

How much cold hard cash do you think you need
to get you through hard times, and how much
do you ever really have?

What is your financial safety net?

What part of your financial situation scares
you the most?

What could the IRS get you on if they really looked closely?

You get to set the tax percentages for lower, middle, and upper class. What would the income divisions be, and what percentage tax would you have each pay?

What is the most you would pay for an autograph of a hero of yours, without the chance of selling it for profit?

What cheap item have you purchased with the hope
that someday it will be worth a mint?

What one item in your life has increased in value
the most since the day you bought it?

What is the most you would spend on an anniversary present, or special anniversary night out?

B

Your loved one suddenly takes out a large insurance policy on you. What do you think?

f

When has your greed gotten you into big trouble?

¢

Who would you turn to to organize your finances right now if you could?

What ad campaign overall has been the most
effective in getting you to spend money?

If you were to leave all your money to a charity
to fight one disease, which would it be?

If you were to get married, or remarried, how much
would you spend on the whole affair?

What would you consider to be the
perfect prenuptial agreement?

When has money earned you respect?

How much money can you spend without feeling as if you need to ask your spouse about it first?

How do your fears about money hold you back from doing something you want to do in life?

What business would you risk your own financial security to go into?

What company do you know you could take over and make a mint running?

Who, of people you know, do you predict will earn
the most money in their lifetime?

دیال

Who that you know will be the next to file bankruptcy?

What is the most money you have held in your hands?

Whose parents of someone you know have manipulated them most with their money?

You have just learned that you have lost all your money. What is the first thing you do?

What percentage of your salary would you sacrifice to solve global warming?

Warren Buffett calls and is willing to answer any one question. What do you ask?

Better with money: men or women?

If you got divorced right now, what would
the fair division of assets be?

Do you trust your mate on money issues
one hundred percent?

Are prenuptial agreements essential?

If you were to assign a value to an hour of your free time, what would it be?

If you earned $10,000 more a year, how would it change your life?

If you earned $100,000 more a year, how would your life change?

If you had to suddenly save $500 per week, how would you do it?

Quick, name three things that matter more than money.
Now quick, name three more.

Would you sell an organ? For how much?

Would you rent your womb?

If you were going to sell your soul, what is the minimum you would ask?

Does being around people with significantly more money than you inspire you or depress you?

If you spend time with a friend who has significantly less money, do you act differently?

Could you be best friends with someone who was significantly wealthier than you?

You find out a friend is good at cheating on his taxes. Do you have more respect for him, or less?

You are out to dinner with friends and have agreed to split the bill evenly before ordering. Someone orders the most expensive meal on the menu. What do you do?

You go to a new restaurant and discover the menu you have been handed has no prices. What do you do?

When does a child living at home become a freeloader?

ℰ

When does a parent living in their children's home
become a freeloader?

When have you gotten a gift that was so cheap
it was offensive?

A friend gives you a coin to take to Vegas and pop into a
slot machine. It hits big. Do you give them the money?

Between you and your spouse, who is the most curious
about how much other people make?

At what point is it necessary to start saving
for retirement?

Do you think your spouse spends too much or too little?

How much do you budget for vacation each year?
And your partner?

What would you pay to find out the exact date
and time you will pass away?

Do you get paid what you deserve for what you do?

WASHINGTON

Whose gift of money would you automatically refuse?

Should money determine how many children you have?

What thing did you splurge on that you knew you shouldn't have, but will never regret?

The person of your dreams is auctioning off a "night out together" for a charity event. What would you be willing to bid?

How much would you pay as a reward
for your pet to be returned?

What would you guess you spend eating out
per month?

What is the hot stock to watch right now?

Who do you know who shops too much?

How well have you organized your finances
in the event of your death?

Sh

What spending habit of your parents bugs you most?

بال

Who in your family will have the most money
when they die?

What have you set for your limit of personal debt?

E

What frivolous thing do you happily spend
money on?

Would you secretly check your fiancée/fiancé's credit rating?

At what stage of a relationship is it OK to open
a joint bank account?

£

A friend files for divorce, asking for more than half of
the assets because her spouse cheated on her. Fair?

Generally speaking, has money been a force for good or for evil in history?

If the government asked you to nominate a new face
to go on the dollar bill, who would you name, other
than yourself?

§

If you could decide to put anything on our coinage other
than In God We Trust, what would it be?

Would you rather be given money, or given the chance to make money on your own?

If a family member told you he/she suddenly came into a hundred thousand dollars, but couldn't tell you how, what would you think?

If your spouse told you she/he needed ten thousand dollars, but never to ask them why, how would you react?

Would you lend money to a family member if they were losing their house in the mortgage crisis?

f

Your sibling, who earns more than you but never saves, asks you for the equivalent of your child's college tuition for a major operation. What do you do?

Someone creates a fortune through questionable means,
but uses it for good. Is that acceptable?

¢

You find out your Christmas bonus came from dirty
money. How much does it bug you?

R

A friend suddenly comes into big money.
Are you happy or jealous?

You win the lottery. Do you take it in one lump payment, or spread it out over thirty years?

How much do you think an inheritance should be taxed?

Who can you most easily manipulate with money?

You're the richest person in the country—what monument do you build to yourself?

Can you save your way to wealth?

Does a woman with money seem more attractive?

When you see an old, unattractive man with a gorgeous young woman on his arm, do you assume she's only with him because he's rich?

Who of all the people you know deserves to earn more for what they do?

Who do you know who could earn a mint if they put their mind to it, but are not interested in doing it?

Who of all the people you know has the worst financial luck?

What indulgence would you love to treat someone with,
if you could afford it?

Do you think children should be taught about money
early, or spared from the issue for as long as possible?

Looking back at various points in life, do you
wish you had saved more?

Does modern society overvalue money?

A guy takes you on a first date, the bill comes, he says, "twenty-six dollars each." Offended?

∮

If your date spends a lot on dinner, do you feel obliged to sleep with him or her?

Do you more readily buy products from a company knowing that it donates to charity?

What career would you have considered if it paid more?

Is it wrong for a company to try to market to kids?

"It takes money to make money." If someone
loaned you money to make more, how would you do it?

Who of your friends has been screwed out of money
in a divorce settlement?

Who made out the best?

Who do you suspect has married purely
for money?

How much do you live for the moment financially?

H

How would you finish the phrase, If only everyone
would spend less money on . . . ?

F

If you were to finish the phrase, If only people would
spend more money on . . . , what would you say?

Is there such a thing as too much money?

What gadget are you truly happy you spent
the money to buy?

How much would you want spent on your funeral
if it happened tomorrow, and who would you
want to pay for it?

In what ways are you superstitious when it
comes to money?

You have been asked to be the bridesmaid for a friend's wedding and it is going to cost you a fortune. How do you deal?

Sh

A colleague at work gets you an expensive and unexpected birthday gift. Their birthday comes along one month after yours. You did not plan on getting them a gift at all. What do you do?

What private club would you join if a friend agreed to fund it for you?

What percentage of your tax dollars do you want to go to the spending on the military?

What charity is it impossible for you to say no to when they solicit money?

How has the attitude about money of your generation been different from the attitude of your parents' generation?

A song becomes an overnight hit single. Who should get the most in royalties, the person who wrote the song or the person who sings the song?

A friend borrows your car and has an accident. Insurance will cover the damage, but your premium will go up a lot the following year. Do you ask the friend for money?

How long would you support your significant other
if they lost their job?

If your boyfriend/girlfriend told you that they always would expect to have separate bank accounts, even if you were married, what would you think?

A couple files separation papers and agrees to split their assets 50/50 when the divorce comes through. In the meantime, one person's parents pass away, leaving them a fortune. Should that get split too?

Two siblings graduate from high school together and one decides to go to college, and the parents pay the way. The other becomes a truck driver and asks the parents if they will give the equivalent amount of money they would have otherwise spent on college to them to help buy a house. What should the parents do?

What one thing do you think you should have a right
to deduct from your taxes but cannot?

If you were given $50,000 to go on the vacation of your
dreams, where would you go?

When has "using other people's money" worked
well for you?

When do you pretend to have more money than you do?

Would you rather be a university graduate who earns an average U.S. income, or a high school dropout who earns six figures?

Which companies should the government bail out, and which should they not?

A fifteen-year-old runs up a bill of $20,000 on his mom's credit card. Should the parents be held liable to pay the bill in full?

How much money would it take to make
your dreams come true?

Looks or money?

F

Rent or buy?

What has been your toughest financial decision to date?

₪

A married father of two also has a child with his mistress. He drops dead. How do you think the money should be divided among the three heirs?

P

Are you part of "Generation Debt"? Whose fault is it that this generation exists at all?

Sh

Are you counting on your parents' inheritance when you plan your financial future?

Knowing that having a well-written will means inheriting more and losing less to Uncle Sam and lawyers, how willing are you to ask your parents about their will, and to discuss the details?

If money were no object, where would you live?

If money were no object, how many hours a week would you work at your current job?

If money were no object, how many nights a week would you eat out?

If one sibling lives near a parent and takes care of them in their old age, should that sibling be entitled to a bigger share of the inheritance when the parent passes away?

When parents write their will, should the child who has six children to raise get more money than the child who has only one child to raise?

How much of the stress in your life would you say
is linked to your money situation?

Would you say that in general you block money
or attract money?

How would your life be different today if your
parents had had twice as much money while you were
growing up?

How often do you check your bank balance?
And your investments?

Do you measure your self-worth with money?

When has giving a donation been most satisfying?

Have you ever met anyone who said they have the
perfect amount of money?

When has money been an obstacle to your well-being?

What is the biggest conflict you have with your family
when it comes to money?

How much control would you say you have over your
ability to earn money?

What is your definition of a millionaire?

What makes money sexy?

If you totaled all your investments and subtracted all your debt, how would your finances look?

P

If you had an extra $300 a month to improve your mental and physical health, how would you spend it?

Sh

Would making more money help your relationship with someone right now?

Is your weight linked in any way to your financial status?

ريال

Are smart people richer overall?

Have you ever lied to your parents to get them to give you money?

In the modern couple, who should foot the bill for the wedding?

Would you stash money secretly if your spouse was overspending?

Would you take a second job for a year to pay off your credit card debt?

What is the highest-paying job you could
get right now?

Which of your investments are the closest to
recession proof?

What would your rules be for giving money
to welfare recipients?

What financial mistake did your parents make
that you won't?

What is the least amount of money you would
bend over to pick up in the street?

Should the person who makes the most money
in a relationship be the one who calls the shots on
how to spend it?

For you, is there a contradiction between religious faith
and seeking financial wealth?

Is money a burden?

About the Authors

Evelyn McFarlane was born in New York. She studied architecture in New York and painting in Italy. She currently lives in Florence, where she writes and paints. She is the mother of an eight-year-old child.

James Saywell is an architect and writer living in Hong Kong and Tuscany.

About the Type

This book was set in Bodoni, a typeface designed by Giambattista Bodoni (1740–1813), the renowned Italian printer and type designer. Bodoni originally based his letter forms on those of the Frenchman Fournier, and created his type to have beautiful contrasts between light and dark.